The Sandbridge

WALTZ AND SLOW AIR COLLECTION

ARRANGEMENTS FOR THE
HAMMERED DULCIMER

By Ken Kolodner

Nine years ago, I launched a weeklong retreat in Sandbridge Beach, Virginia for hammered dulcimer players. I started "Sandbridge" to provide an intensive learning environment in a relaxed setting. Since its inception, Sandbridge has evolved into three weeklong workshops that draw 50 intermediate and advanced players from around the U.S. and beyond. This collection draws heavily from arrangements developed at Sandbridge and over the course of my 30-year career as a hammered dulcimer performer and instructor. Following "The Sandbridge Dance Tune Collection," the second collection focuses on a slower repertoire such as waltzes, airs, O'Carolan and marches.

MEL BAY ®

1 2

Visit us on the Web at www.melbay.com — E-mail us at email@melbay.com

The Sandbridge
WALTZ AND SLOW AIR COLLECTION

Arrangements of traditional and original waltzes, slow airs, marches, O'Carolan and more. The repertoire draws from the U.S., Ireland, Scotland, Cape Breton, England, Shetland Islands, Finland, Sweden and Israel. Includes basic tunes and one or more arrangements for each tune, offering a wide range of levels of complexity. Backup and harmony parts are provided for many of the pieces.

To order copies of the book, please contact:

Ken Kolodner
3806 Fenchurch Rd.
Baltimore, MD 21218
410-746-8387
www.kenkolodner.com
kenkolodner@aol.com

TABLE OF CONTENTS

APPENDICES

ACKNOWLEDGEMENTS

This book would not have been possible without all those who have taken lessons or workshops from me, motivating me to write out many hundreds of arrangements. Much thanks goes to all those musicians from whom I have learned these tunes and countless others. Thanks to Kathy Sanderson for her invaluable assistance in putting this book together. And to my family, Alison, Bradley and Hillary!

INTRODUCTION

How I chose the tunes

In "The Sandbridge Dance Tune Collection," I selected mostly traditional and some original "fiddle tunes" including reels, jigs, hornpipes and polkas. The companion collection ("The Sandbridge Waltz and Slow Air Collection") draws largely from my slower repertoire of airs, waltzes, O'Carolan and marches. In this book, I include a healthy dose of Celtic (mostly Irish and Scottish), American, and Québécois tunes, as well as some traditional pieces from around the world (England, Israel, Sweden, Finland, Chile). For this collection, to keep the repertoire focused, I chose not to include hymns, Christmas tunes, popular and classical music but will save those for a future collection. These pieces represent many of my favorites!

I selected the music partially to represent a wide range of level of complexity. But even for some of the simpler tunes, I often present ideas that range from very simple and easy to execute to considerably more complex. For some of the tunes, I present multiple arrangements again ranging from very simple to considerably more complex. My intent is to present tunes and arranging ideas appropriate for a wide range of playing abilities.

Please consider the written notation as a guide. Ultimately, it really helps to hear examples of the arrangements. Over my thirty plus years of playing the hammered dulcimer, I've recorded or performed many of these tunes. Jump on YouTube and look for me! If you have some of my recordings or instructional CDs, please listen to the tune that you are considering learning. (You may refer to the index of tunes in this book to see which tunes I have recorded.)

Backup and harmony parts

My main focus in this book is on solo arrangements but I have included a backup and/or one or more harmony parts for about a third of the tunes. Many of the harmony parts are likely more appropriate for an instrument capable of sustaining a note, like a fiddle or flute. I included them hoping that you will share them with others with whom you may play.

Over the years, I have learned so much more from developing accompaniment parts than from developing leads. In fact, backup is my favorite place to be, working in the chord progressions and in rhythm. My hope is that you will learn a lot about the tunes if you spend some time exploring the backup parts. I improvise frequently in creating a backup just as I do while playing my arrangements. But what I have written down should offer a good start.

My three arranging approaches: Individual techniques, the full model and the kitchen sink

I like to approach teaching arranging using three general methods. I have presented many examples of each of these in this volume.

First is a technique-driven approach where I use only one idea and present it in the entire tune. The idea here is to master that one idea so that it will be available to use in a wide variety of tunes. While using just a single idea can sometimes be a bit tedious to play, one idea can be quite effective. For example, I use only two-note chords in one version of *Fanny Power*. In this version, I demonstrate the use of two-note chords to create ascending and descending bass lines and to separate the harmony in physical distance from the melody. I might not play the tune ever with *only* two-note chords, but I think that you will find this version surprisingly successful. In *Southwind*, I present three versions that each use a single idea, using "two-note chords," "three-note chords," and "fills". I also include a more adventurous version that combines ideas. In practice, I rarely play a tune using only one idea, but it is excellent practice to be able to master each idea separately. Ultimately, by mastering each idea, my hope is that you will be able to create your own arrangement that incorporates each technique.

In my second approach, I present a full model of how I might play the tune at least one time through. Here I use a variety of ideas to embellish the tune. There are many examples of this approach such as *Bonny at Morn, The Down Home Waltz* and *The Clock Waltz*. Although I typically only present one pass of the tune, these "full model" arrangements work as stand-alone arrangements, unlike the third approach that I offer in the book.

In this last approach, I cram in as many ideas as I can on a single page. I often write out the repeats of the A and B parts and present a new idea in each couple of measures. I like to think of this as the "kitchen sink" approach that is meant to be a collection of ideas. Rarely would I play all these ideas together as it would likely obscure and overwhelm the tune. My goal is that you will eventually be able to pick and choose from the many ideas to create multiple arrangements of the tune.

Caution: always learn just the melody and keep moving!

This is an obvious point, but so often I see folks have nailed a complicated arrangement and the listener can barely tell what the tune is. My thinking is that you should always be able to play the basic tune with no embellishments. First, it can be refreshing and rewarding to play through the basic tune simply, and focus on phrasing and musicality. Second, you should have some concept how the ideas were developed by always keeping the basic tune in sight.

A further word of encouragement: do not focus on your mistakes. Especially as you begin to add ideas and master the arrangements, try to practice without "correcting." It is easy to fall in the trap of trying to master an arrangement and sacrificing the flow of the tune. If a particular idea seems too difficult, simplify. Ultimately, some wrong notes do not matter, but losing the rhythm does. Learning to never stop is a difficult lesson, but the most important one.

Using the arrangements

I hesitate to use the word "arrangement" to describe what I have presented in this volume. Many of the "arrangements" are collections of ideas from which I hope you will learn to incorporate into your own new arrangements. In this collection, when I write "arranging ideas," I have written down a collection of ideas that I could fit on one page. I did not intend that the entire page be played exactly as written. Rather, I have condensed into one page a variety of ideas that could perhaps be thought of as a library of ideas that you might use in different passes of the tune. For example, I would never play *Carolan's Draught: arranging ideas* as my first pass through the tune or any pass through the tune. Rather, I might pull in some of those ideas as I play the tune multiple times. In contrast, when I have written "arrangement #1," or simply "arrangement," I think of this as a stand-alone presentation of the tune that I might play in total.

In "The Sandbridge Dance Tune Collection," I included a discussion of the most common ideas that I present in the transcriptions in both books. For some of the tunes in "The Sandbridge Waltz and Slow Air Collection," I have included annotated descriptions of the ideas in some of the arrangements such as *Bonny at Morn: arrangement*, *The Down Home Waltz* and *Polska: arranging ideas.* It may be informative to refer to the discussion in "The Dance Tune Collection" and to look at these annotated arrangements in order to understand the ideas and notation.

I hope you enjoy the tunes!

Avenging and Bright ("Crooghan a Venee"): melody with accompaniment

Ireland (Lyrics by Thomas Moore (1779-1852)): Arranged by © Ken Kolodner

The B part is often played with all minor chords. However, I prefer moving to the "relative" major chords for the first half of the B part, setting up the movement back to minor chords in the second half of the B part.

Avenging and Bright ("Crooghan a Venee"): arrangement

Ireland (Lyrics by Thomas Moore (1779-1852)): Arranged by © Ken Kolodner

Bethany Beach

Recorded on Ken and Brad Kolodner's "Otter Creek" (2011)

Bethany Beach: arrangement #1

Recorded on Brad and Ken Kolodner's "Otter Creek" (2011)

Bethany Beach: arrangement #2

Recorded on Ken and Brad Kolodner's "Otter Creek" (2011)

Black Tail Canyon Waltz

Recorded on Ken Kolodner's "Journey to the Heartland" (2005)

August, 2004: © Ken Kolodner

Black Tail Canyon Waltz: arranging ideas

Recorded on Ken Kolodner's "Journey to the Heartland" (2005)

August, 2004: © Ken Kolodner

Play with swing eighth notes. Most of the arrangement is fairly straightforward, primarily using simple arpeggio fills, valley rolls, the occasional two and three note chords, along with a few hammered and bounced triplets now and again. Add some dynamics and you are on your way.

Bonny At Morn: melody, harmony, accompaniment

Recorded on Mark Grobner and Ken Kolodner's "SunRise" (2011)

Northumberland: Arranged by © Ken Kolodner

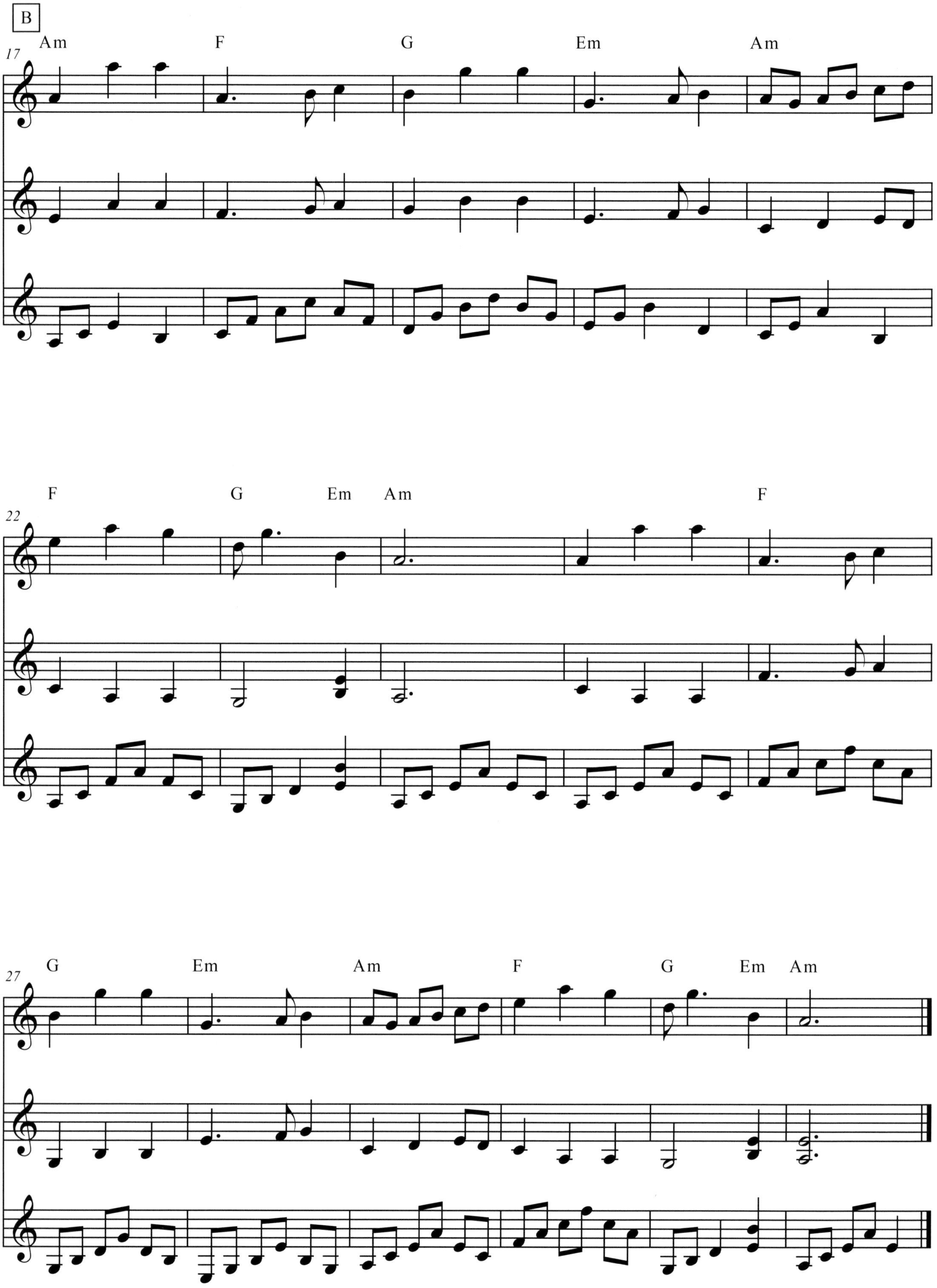
B
17
Am
F
G
Em
Am
22
F
G
Em
Am
F
27
G
Em
Am
F
G
Em
Am

Bonny At Morn: arranging ideas

Recorded on Mark Grobner and Ken Kolodner's "SunRise" (2011)

Northumberland: Arranged by © Ken Kolodner

Carolan's Draught

Recorded on Ken Kolodner's "Walking Stones" (1997, re-released 2006)
with Robin Bullock and Laura Risk

Turlough O'Carolan (Ireland): Arranged by © Ken Kolodner

Carolan's Draught: arranging ideas

Recorded on Ken Kolodner's "Walking Stones" (1997, re-released 2006)
with Robin Bullock and Laura Risk

Turlough O'Carolan: Arranged by © Ken Kolodner

23
C D C Em Am
26
C Bm Am G D Em D C D
30
Em D G D7 G
33
D B7/D♯ Em C Em E♭
36
CMaj7 G B7/F♯ Em Bm/D
39
C D C Em Am
42
C Bm Am G D Em D
3 3 3 3
45
C D Em D G D7 G

Caspian Lake: with harmony

Recorded on Ken Kolodner's "Walking Stones" (1997, re-released 2006) with Robin Bullock & Laura Risk and on "Hammered Dulcimer Arrangements: Waltzes and Slow Tunes: Volume I" (2005)

August, 1995 © Ken Kolodner

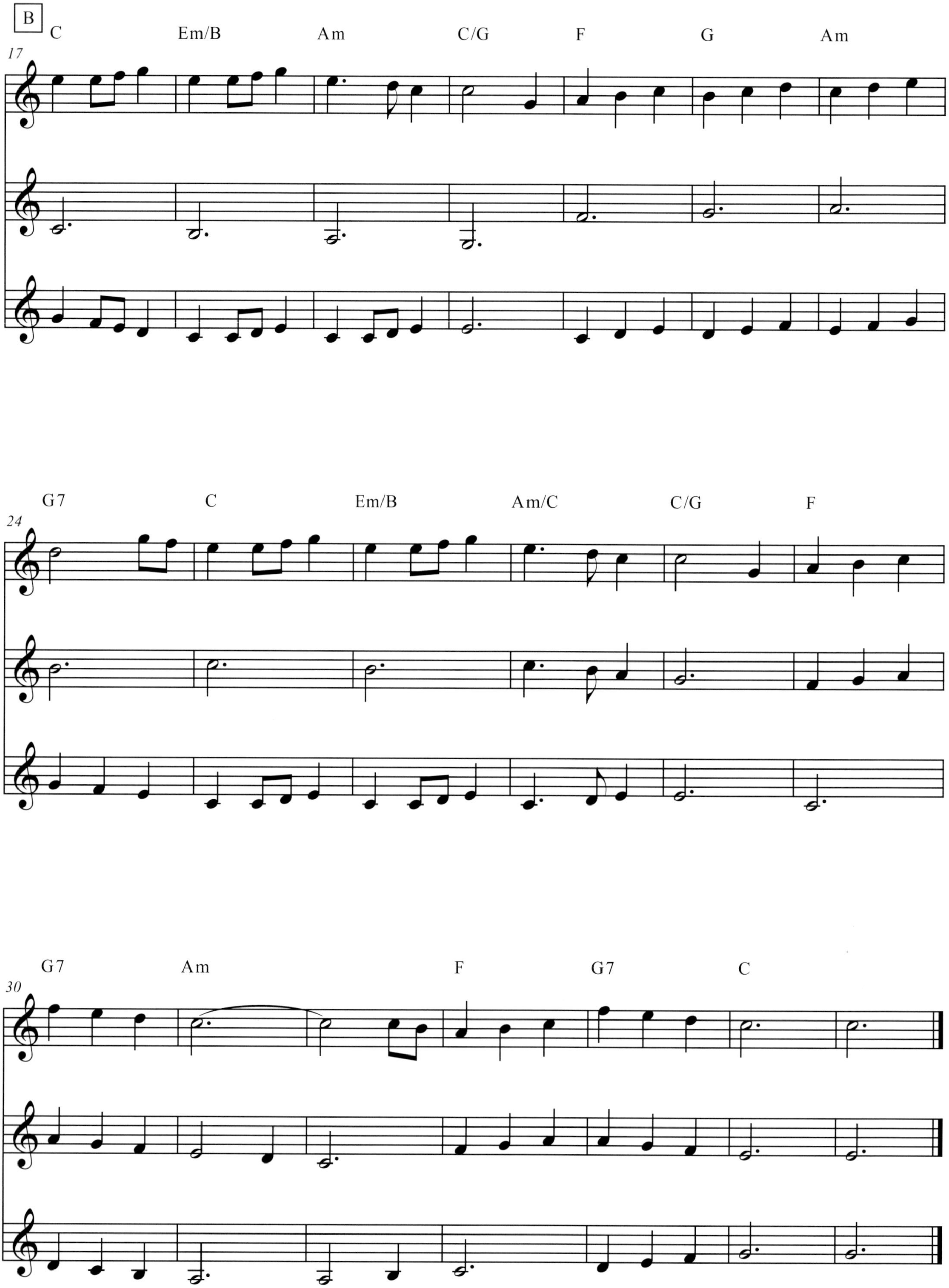
B
C
Em/B
Am
C/G
F
G
Am
17
G7
C
Em/B
Am/C
C/G
F
24
G7
Am
F
G7
C
30

Caspian Lake: arrangement

Recorded on Ken Kolodner's "Walking Stones" (1997, re-released 2006) and
on "Hammered Dulcimer Arrangements: Waltzes and Slow Tunes, Volume I" (2005)

August, 1995 © Ken Kolodner

"The Clock Waltz" (Valse Clog Guillemette)

Recorded on Ken Kolodner's "Walking Stones" (1997, re-released 2006) with Laura Risk and Robin Bullock, and on "Hammered Dulcimer Arrangements: Waltzes Vol II" (2005)

Joseph Guillemette (1886-1950) Quebec: Arranged by © Ken Kolodner

In this beautiful piece, I use many accent shifts which significantly changes the feel of the tune. The shifts provide a significant element of surprise and enhanced musicality. This tune is usually played in Bm but works well in Em.

The "Clock Waltz" (Valse Clog Guillemette): arranging ideas

Recorded on Ken Kolodner's "Walking Stones" (1997, re-released 2006) and
on "Hammered Dulcimer Arrangements: Waltzes Vol II" (2005)

Joseph Guillemette (Quebec): Arranged by © Ken Kolodner

Coleman's March

Recorded on Ken Kolodner's "Journey to the Heartland" (2005) and on
"Hammered Dulcimer Arrangements: Waltzes and Slow Tunes Volume I" (2005)

U.S.: Arranged by © Ken Kolodner

Play with some swing.

Coleman's March: arrangement #1

Recorded on Ken Kolodner's "Journey to the Heartland" (2005) and on
"Hammered Dulcimer Arrangements: Waltzes and Slow Tunes Volume I" (2005)

U.S.: Arranged by © Ken Kolodner

Note the use of some chord subs, simple bass lines using two-note chords, valley rolls & grace notes. There are very few modifications of the melody in this arrangement. Play with a slight swing.

Coleman's March: arrangement #2

Recorded on Ken Kolodner's "Journey to the Heartland" (2005) and on
"Hammered Dulcimer Arrangements: Waltz and Slow Tunes Volume I" (2005)

U.S.: Arranged by © Ken Kolodner

Play dynamically and with a little bit of swing.

Cowboy Waltz

Recorded on Ken and Brad Kolodner's "Skipping Rocks" (2013)

U.S.: Arranged by © Ken Kolodner

Play with swing eighth notes

Cowboy Waltz: arranging ideas

Recorded on Ken and Brad Kolodner's "Skipping Rocks" (2013)

U.S.: Arranged by © Ken Kolodner

The Cradle Song: hand separation

Recorded on Mark Grobner and Ken Kolodner's "SunRise" (2011)

Scott Skinner (Scotland): Arranged by © Ken Kolodner

Da Auld Resting Chair

Tom Anderson (Shetland Islands): Arranged by © Ken Kolodner

Da Auld Resting Chair: arrangement #1

Tom Anderson (Shetland Islands): Arranged by © Ken Kolodner

Da Auld Resting Chair: more arranging ideas

Tom Anderson (Shetland Islands): Arranged by © Ken Kolodner

Da Slockit Licht: with harmony

Recorded on Helicon's "Helicon" (1987) with Ken Kolodner, Chris Norman and Robin Bullock

Tom Anderson (Shetland Island): Arranged by © Ken Kolodner

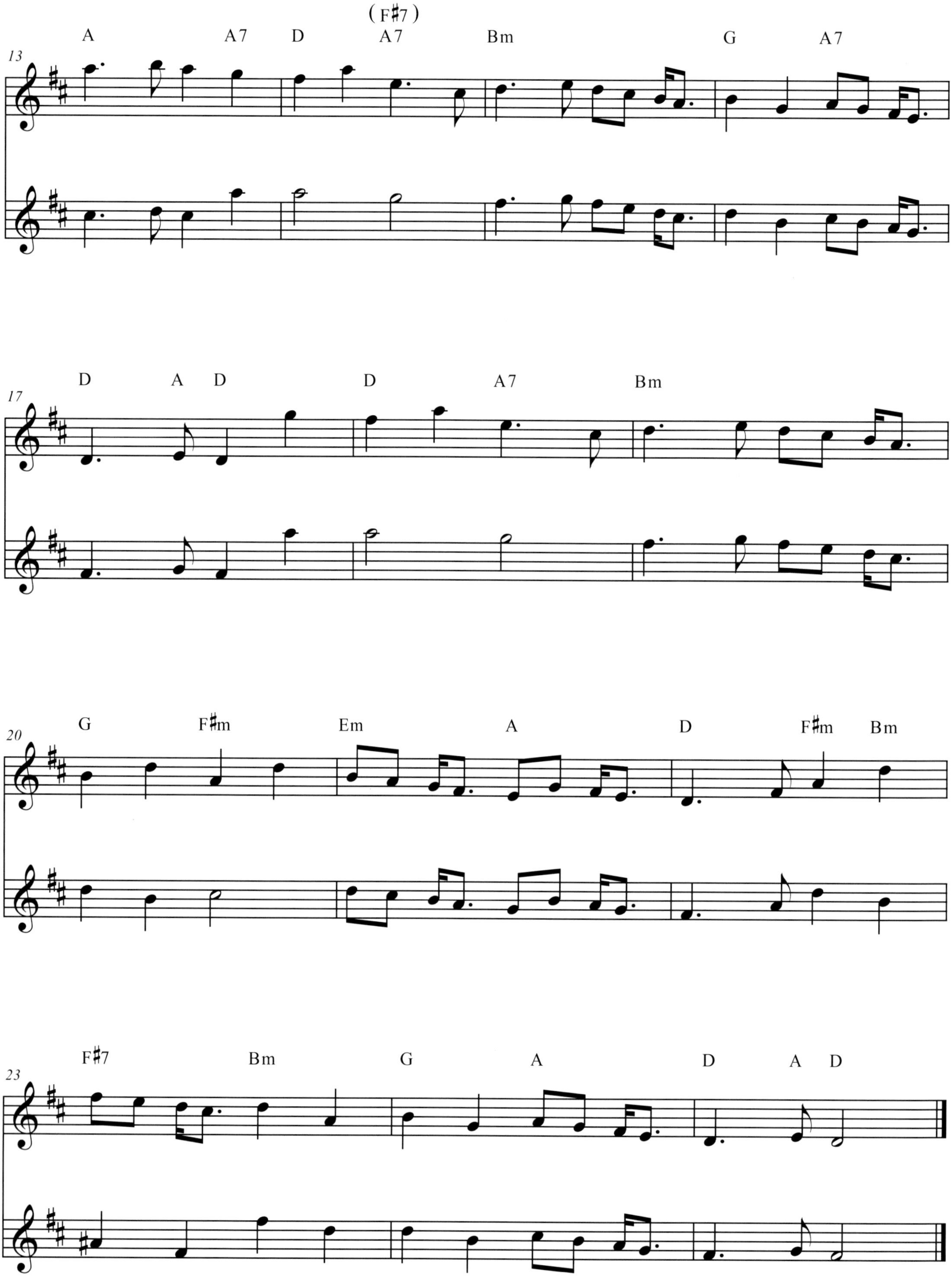
(F♯7)
A A7 D A7 Bm G A7
13
D A D D A7 Bm
17
G F♯m Em A D F♯m Bm
20
F♯7 Bm G A D A D
23

Da Slockit Licht: arrangement

Recorded on Helicon's "Helicon" (1987) with Ken Kolodner, Chris Norman and Robin Bullock

Tom Anderson: Arranged by © Ken Kolodner

Dermott O'Dowd: melody, accompaniment

O'Carolan: Arranged by © Ken Kolodner

Dermott O'Dowd: arrangement #1

O'Carolan: Arranged © by Ken Kolodner

Dermott O'Dowd: more arranging ideas

O'Carolan: Arranged © by Ken Kolodner

The Down Home Waltz:
melody, arrangement, accompaniment

Recorded on Ken Kolodner's "Journey to the Heartland" (2005) and
"Hammered Dulcimer Arrangements: Waltzes and Slow Tunes, Volume I" (2005)

Buck White (U.S.): Arranged by © Ken Kolodner

Note suggested accent markings—I provide these occasionally as a reminder to use accent shifts.

Measure one combines an introductory 4 note rapid arpeggio followed by a triplet falling into an accent shift to the "3" count
Measure two begins with a valley roll followed by a drone note
Measure three begins with a 3 note chord and an accent shift to the 2 count
Measure four uses an arpeggio fill
Measure five combines a flam followed by an arpeggio fill followed by an accent shift to the "and" of the 2 count

Measure six adds a syncopation on the "and" of the one count. Measure seven incorporates a chromatic to mimic a pitch bend
Measure eight adds another syncopation. Measures 9-12 re-cycle the same arrangement used in 1-4.
Measure 13 (below): 2 note chord. Measure 14 adds a syncopation and a hint of dissonance that is quickly resolved.
Measure 15 adds a bounced triplet with a small melodic run. Measure 16 moves into the B part of the tune with a small chromatic run. Measure 17 adds an arpeggios fill and continues with the chromatic run. I also introduce a chord sub of A7 which moves to the D chord. This illustrates the first of several "secondary dominants" used in the B section.

Measure 18 uses a simple arpeggio fill.

Measure 19 continues with another secondary dominant, this time a B7 chord (subbed in for a Bm7) which moves the tune strongly to an Em. A simple arppeggio works well to accomplish the chord change. Measure 20 uses an arpeggio fill. Measure 21 continues the use of secondary dominants with a 2-note chord and a chromatic run to move to an A7 chord in measure 22-23. A drone is used in measure 23. We move to a D7 chord in measure 24 which needs resolution back to a G chord in measure 25, where we return to the A part theme. However, some different ideas are now used beginning with a high drone on a B.

Measure 26 uses simple two note chords using "6ths." Measure 27 follows with a three note chord. Measure 28 uses an arpeggio fill with a chromatic. Measures 29-32 use the same arrangement as the ending of the A part.

Note on backup: The accompaniment used here should be phrased dynamically to follow the lead. Also, the arpeggios and runs used are far too dense if each note is played "as is." Try to drop out some of the notes to allow the lead to breathe and to phrase the eighth notes by playing lightly, yet provide a solid pulse. I play an accompaniment that approximates what is written here on my recording "Journey to the Heartland." It will be instructive to hear this in practice.

Emma: melody, arrangement, and accompaniment

Finland: Arranged by © Ken Kolodner

B
11
Dm G7 C
Dm Dm/C G7/B C
14
Am B7 E7
Am B E7
3 3 3
17
1. 2.
Am E7 A7 Am
Am E7 A7 Am E7 Am

Erev Shel Shoshanim (Evening of Roses): melody with harmony, arpeggio accompaniment

Recorded on Helicon's "A Winter Solstice Celebration" (1999) and on
"Hammered Dulcimer Arrangements for Waltzes and Slow Tunes: Vol I" (2005)

Arranged by © Ken Kolodner

The melody works well in the upper octave. Play the arpeggio accompaniment in the lowest available octave.

Erev Shel Shoshanim (Evening of Roses):
hand separation

Recorded on "A Winter Solstice Celebration with Helicon"(1999) and as described on
"Hammered Dulcimer Arrangements: Waltzes and Slow Tunes Volume I" (2005)

Moshe Dor (Israel): Arranged by © Ken Kolodner

Play right hand in lowest octave possible.

Erev Shel Shoshanim (Evening of Roses): arrangement #1

Recorded on Helicon's "A Winter Solstice Celebration" and on
"Hammered Dulcimer Arrangements for Waltzes and Slow Tunes: Vol I" (2005)

Moshe Dor (Israel): Arranged by © Ken Kolodner

Erev Shel Shoshanim (Evening of Roses): more arranging ideas

Recorded on Helicon's "A Winter Solstice Celebration with Helicon" (1999) and as described on "Hammered Dulcimer Arrangements: Waltzes and Slow Tunes, Volume I" (2005)

Moshe Dor (Israel): Arranged by © Ken Kolodner

Fair Hills of Killen

Recorded on Mark Grobner and Ken Kolodner's "Sunrise" (2011)

Peadar O'Doirnin (Ireland): Arranged by © Ken Kolodner

Fair Hills of Killen: arrangement

Recorded on Mark Grobner and Ken Kolodner's "Sunrise" (2011)

Peadar O'Doirnin (Ireland): Arranged by © Ken Kolodner

Fanny Power: melody with harmony

Recorded on Chris Norman and Ken Kolodner's "Daybreak" (1985, re-released in 2010)

Turlough O'Carolan (Ireland): Arranged by © Ken Kolodner

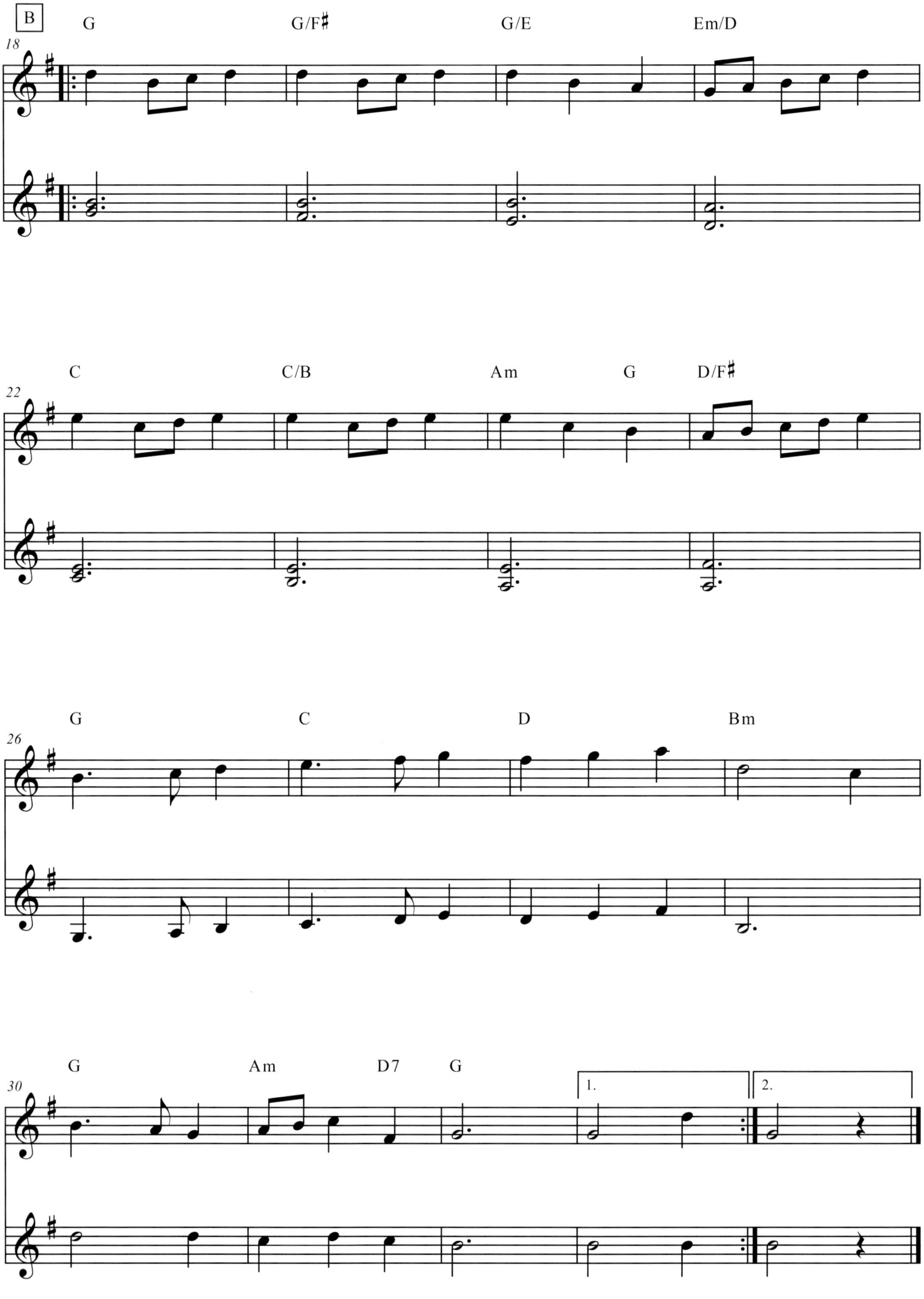
B
18
G G/F♯ G/E Em/D
22
C C/B Am G D/F♯
26
G C D Bm
30
G Am D7 G
1.
2.

Fanny Power: arrangement using two note chords

Recorded on Chris Norman and Ken Kolodner's "Daybreak" (1985, re-released in 2010)

Turlough O'Carolan (Ireland): Arranged by © Ken Kolodner

Slash chords are used above to indicate the bass line (i.e. the note to the right of the slash is to be used as the bass line). I have written out this tune so that it is completely playable on a 12/11 instrument. However, on larger instruments, I recommend dropping some of the chord notes an octave lower. E.g., in the A part, starting in measure 2-4, play the F♯, E and D one octave lower. Also, play the grace note "F♯" one octave lower. This arrangement offers an example of the successful use of only simple two-note chords with no other techniques. It may not be complex but it is very effective.

Fanny Power: arrangement using "fills"

Recorded on Chris Norman and Ken Kolodner's "Daybreak" (1985, re-released in 2010)

Turlough O'Carolan (Ireland): Arranged by © Ken Kolodner

Fanny Power: more arranging ideas

Recorded on Chris Norman and Ken Kolodner's "Daybreak" (1985, re-released in 2010)

Turlough O'Carolan (Ireland): Arranged by © Ken Kolodner

Far Away

Peter Jung: Arranged by © Ken Kolodner

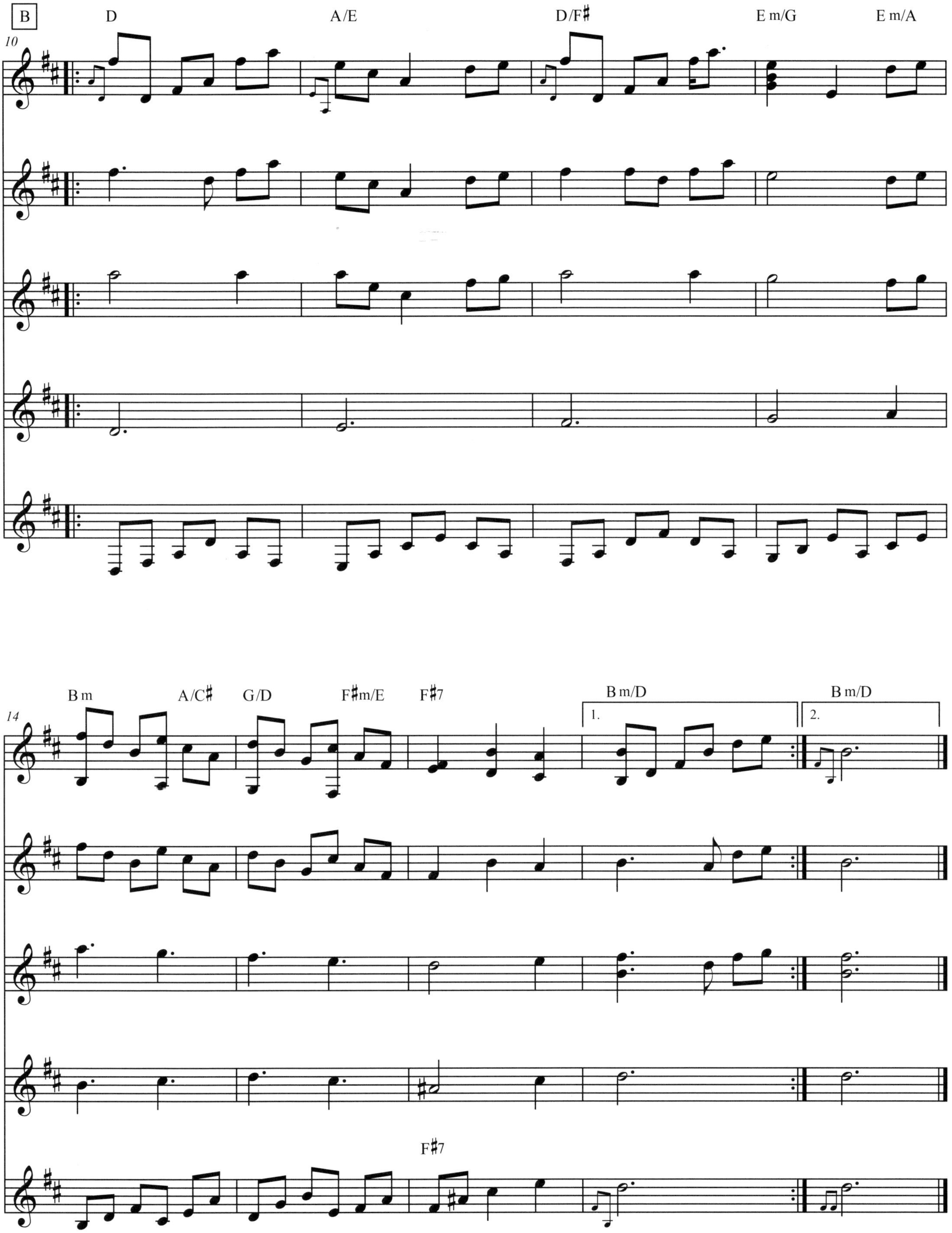
B
D
A/E
D/F♯
E m/G
E m/A
10
B m
A/C♯
G/D
F♯m/E
F♯7
B m/D
1.
B m/D
2.
14
F♯7

For Ireland I'd Dare Not Tell Her Name

Recorded on Ken Kolodner and Elke Baker's "Out of the Wood" (2011)
and on Mark Grobner and Ken Kolodner's "SunRise" (2011)

Ireland: Arranged by © Ken Kolodner

For Ireland I'd Dare Not Tell Her Name: arrangement

Recorded on Ken Kolodner and Elke Baker's "Out of the Wood"(2011) and on
Mark Grobner and Ken Kolodner's "SunRise" (2011)

Ireland: Arranged by © Ken Kolodner

Forvantan: melody with accompaniment

Recorded on Mark Grobner and Ken Kolodner's "Sunrise" (2011)

Hasse Jonnson: Arranged by © Ken Kolodner

Forvantan: arrangement #1

Recorded on Mark Grobner and Ken Kolodner's "Sunrise" (2011)

Hasse Jonnson: Arranged by © Ken Kolodner

Forvantan: arrangement #2

Recorded on Mark Grobner and Ken Kolodner's 2011 release "Sunrise"

Hasse Jonnson: Arranged by © Ken Kolodner

Gentle Eily O'Carol (Eily Gheal Chiun)

Dominick Mongan, Ireland, circa 1750: Arranged by © Ken Kolodner

This beautiful piece can be played in two octaves.

Gentle Eily O'Carol (Eily Gheal Chiun): accompaniment

Dominick Mongan, Ireland, circa 1750: Arranged by © Ken Kolodner

Gentle Eily O'Carol (Eily Gheal Chiun): arrangement

Dominick Mongan, Ireland, circa 1750: Arranged by © Ken Kolodner

Give me Your Hand

Rory Dall O'Cathain (Ireland circa 1570-1650): Arranged by © Ken Kolodner

Play this ending for the last time through.

Give me Your Hand: arrangement #1

Rory Dall O'Cathain (Ireland circa 1570-1650): Arranged by © Ken Kolodner

Give me Your Hand: more arranging ideas

Rory Dall O'Cathain (Ireland circa 1570-1650): Arranged by © Ken Kolodner

Play this ending for the last time through

Hard Times

Stephen Foster: Arranged by © Ken Kolodner

In the "slash chords" above, the notes to the right of the slash indicate the bass line.

Hard Times: arrangement

Stephen Foster: Arranged by © Ken Kolodner

Ian Robertson

Recorded on Ken Kolodner's "Walking Stones" (1997, re-released 2006)
with Laura Risk and Robin Bullock

Tom Anderson (Shetland Islands): Arranged by © Ken Kolodner

Ian Robertson: arrangement

Recorded on Ken Kolodner's "Walking Stones" (1997, re-released 2006)
with Laura Risk and Robin Bullock

Tom Anderson (Shetland Islands): Arranged by © Ken Kolodner

Take your time on this one! Note the use of the secondary dominant chords (C#7, A7 and B7).

Kevin Keegan's

From Ken Kolodner's "Walking Stones" (1997, re-released 2006)
with Laura Risk and Robin Bullock

Ireland: Arranged by © Ken Kolodner

43 D7/F♯ Em7 Bm/D G Am D7 G
C
49 D7 G Bm
53 Em Am
57 C G
61 D G
65 D G Bm
69 Em Am9
73 Am A♯dim7 G Em
78 Am D7 G 1. G 2.

Kevin Keegan's: arranging ideas

Recorded on Ken Kolodner's "Walking Stones" (1997, re-released 2006)
with Laura Risk and Robin Bullock

Ireland: Arranged by © Ken Kolodner

G D7/A Em7/G Bm G Am D7 G
C
D7 No swing G Bm
Em Am
C G
D G No swing
D G Bm
Em Am9
Am A♯dim7 G
Em Am D7 G

La Partida

Recorded on Helicon's "Helicon" (1987) with Chris Norman, Robin Bullock and Ken Kolodner

Victor Jara, Chile: Arranged by © Ken Kolodner

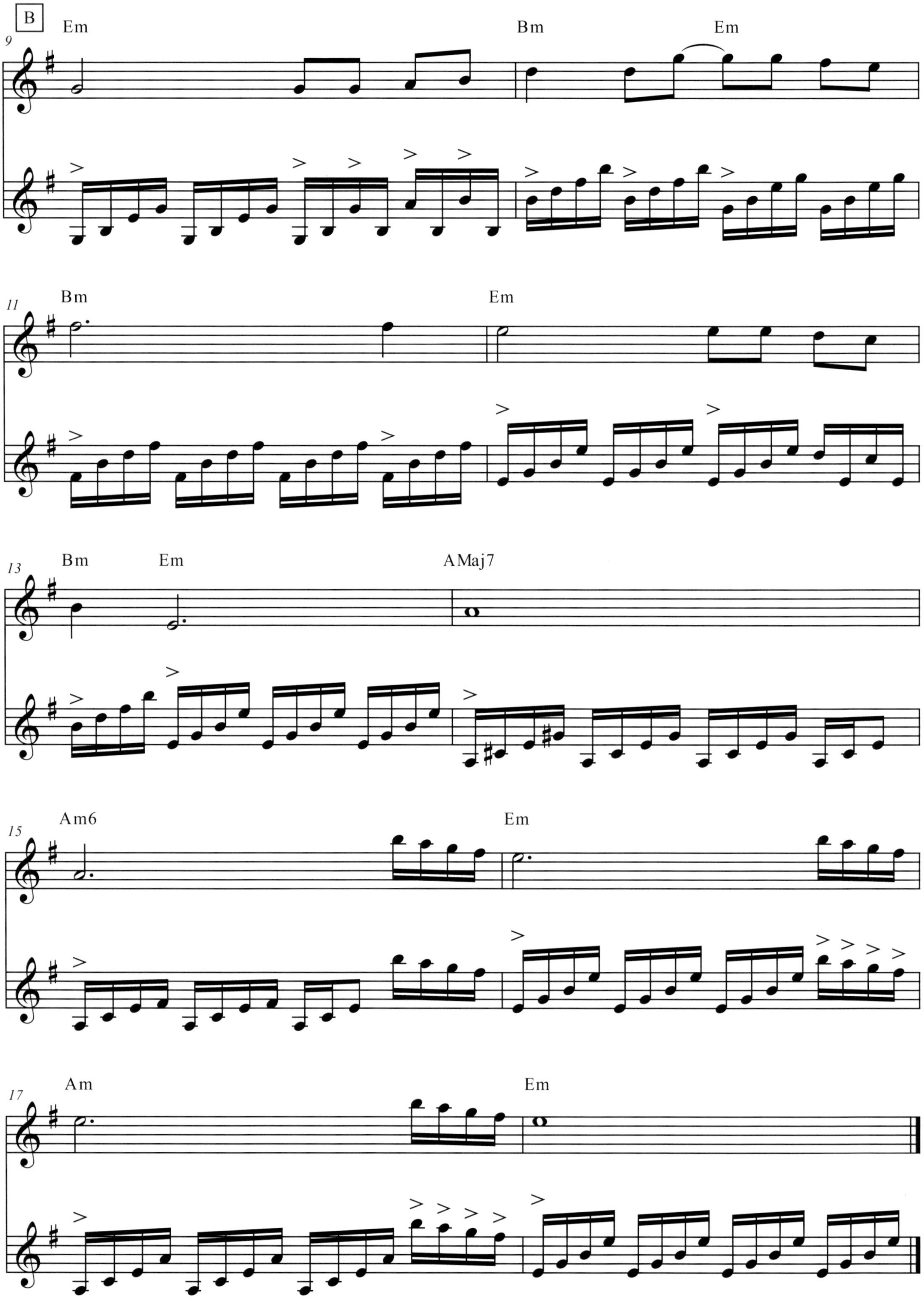
B
9
Em
Bm
Em
11
Bm
Em
13
Bm
Em
AMaj7
15
Am6
Em
17
Am
Em

Lango Lee

Recorded on Ken Kolodner and Elke Baker's "Out of the Wood" (2011)

Scotland from The Gow Collection: Arranged by © Ken Kolodner

Lango Lee: arrangement

Recorded on Ken Kolodner and Elke Baker's "Out of the Wood" (2011)

Scotland from the Gow Collection: Arranged by © Ken Kolodner

The Light Sparrow

Recorded on Ken Kolodner's "Journey to the Heartland" (2005)

Quebec: Arranged by © Ken Kolodner

The Light Sparrow: arrangement

Recorded on Ken Kolodner's "Journey to the Heartland" (2005)

Quebec: Arranged by © Ken Kolodner

Lo Yisa Goy (Lay Down Your Arms)

Israel: Arranged by © Ken Kolodner

Lay Down Your Arms: arrangement

Israel: Arranged by © Ken Kolodner

Loftus Jones

Turlough O'Carolan (Ireland): Arranged by © Ken Kolodner

Loftus Jones: arranging ideas

Turlough O'Carolan (Ireland): Arranged by © Ken Kolodner

MacPherson's Lament: melody, harmony

Recorded on Mark Grobner and Ken Kolodner's "SunRise" (2011)

James MacPherson, Scotland (circa 1700): Arranged by © Ken Kolodner

MacPherson's Lament: two note chords

Recorded on Mark Grobner and Ken Kolodner's "SunRise" (2011)

James MacPherson, Scotland (circa 1700): Arranged by © Ken Kolodner

MacPherson's Lament: three and four note chords

Recorded on Mark Grobner and Ken Kolodner's "SunRise" (2011)

James MacPherson, Scotland (circa 1700): Arranged by © Ken Kolodner

MacPherson's Lament: more arranging ideas

Recorded on Mark Grobner and Ken Kolodner's "SunRise" (2011)

James MacPherson, Scotland (circa 1700): Arranged by © Ken Kolodner

March of the King of Laois

Recorded on Ken Kolodner and Laura Risk's "A Roof for the Rain" (2001) and on
"Hammered Dulcimer Arrangements: Waltzes and Slow Tunes Volume II" (2005)

Ireland: Arranged by © Ken Kolodner

March of the King of Laois: arrangement

Recorded on Ken Kolodner and Laura Risk's "A Roof for the Rain" (2001) and on
"Hammered Dulcimer Arrangements: Waltzes and Slow Tunes Volume II" (2005)

Ireland: Arranged by © Ken Kolodner

The grace notes are played using bounces and dragging your hammer

Typically, I improvise through this section using arpeggios and scales. Here is an example.

94

Margaret Anne Robertson

Recorded on Chris Norman and Ken Kolodner's "Daybreak" (1985, re-released 2010)

Jamieson (Scotland): Arranged by © Ken Kolodner

Margaret Anne Robertson: arranging ideas

Recorded on Chris Norman and Ken Kolodner's "Daybreak" (1985, re-released 2010)

Jamieson (Scotland): Arranged by © Ken Kolodner

My Cape Breton Home

Recorded on Ken Kolodner's "Journey to the Heartland" (2005) and
"Hammered Dulcimer Arrangements: Waltzes and Slow Tunes Vol II" (2005)

Jerry Holland: Arranged by © Ken Kolodner

My Cape Breton Home: Arranging Ideas

Recorded on Ken Kolodner's "Journey to the Heartland" (2005) and on
"Hammered Dulcimer Arrangements: Waltzes and Slow Tunes Volume II" (2005)

Jerry Holland: Arranged by © Ken Kolodner

This arrangement uses three note chords, valley rolls, fills, arpeggios, drones, triplets, melodic runs, chord substitutions and two note chords to create a rising bass line (in the B part). The rising bass line in the B part is quite powerful. It is quite sufficient to use over and over again!

The Orange Rogue

Recorded on Ken Kolodner and Elke Baker's "Out of the Wood" (2011)

Ireland: Arranged by © Ken Kolodner

To accommodate the arrangement, I've suggested hammering where the left hand plays all eighth notes.

The Orange Rogue: arrangement

Recorded on Ken Kolodner and Elke Baker's "Out of the Wood" (2011)

Ireland: Arranged by © Ken Kolodner

In measures 8 and 25, I use the right hammer to play both harmony notes by playing in the valley between the right treble and bass bridge. Measure 17 is a difficult passage. If it doesn't work for you, consider something simpler! Similarly, avoid the triplets if they get in the way of a good flow.

Polska

Sweden: Arranged by © Ken Kolodner

Polska: arranging ideas

Swedish: From Becky Tracy, Arranged by © Ken Kolodner

Prince William

English Country Dance: Arranged by © Ken Kolodner

Prince William: arrangement #1

English Country Dance: Arranged by © Ken Kolodner

Prince William: more arranging ideas

English Country Dance: Arranged by © Ken Kolodner

Return from Fingal

Ireland: Arranged by © Ken Kolodner

Return from Fingal: arrangement

Ireland: Arranged by © Ken Kolodner

Sir Sydney Smith's March

Recorded on Ken Kolodner and Elke Baker's "Out of the Wood" (2011)

James Hook (England): Arranged by © Ken Kolodner

Sir Sydney Smith's: arranging ideas

Recorded on Ken Kolodner and Elke Baker's "Out of the Wood" (2011)

James Hook (England): Arranged by © Ken Kolodner

In measures 33-40, I often improvise using the chord progression. An example is shown in measure 37-38.

Southwind: melody, harmony, arpeggio backup

Ireland: Arranged by© Ken Kolodner

The backup is very "busy" but is good practice for arpeggios. I suggest dropping out some of the notes to give the backup some space. Try playing the arpeggios lightly but emphasize the "one" count.

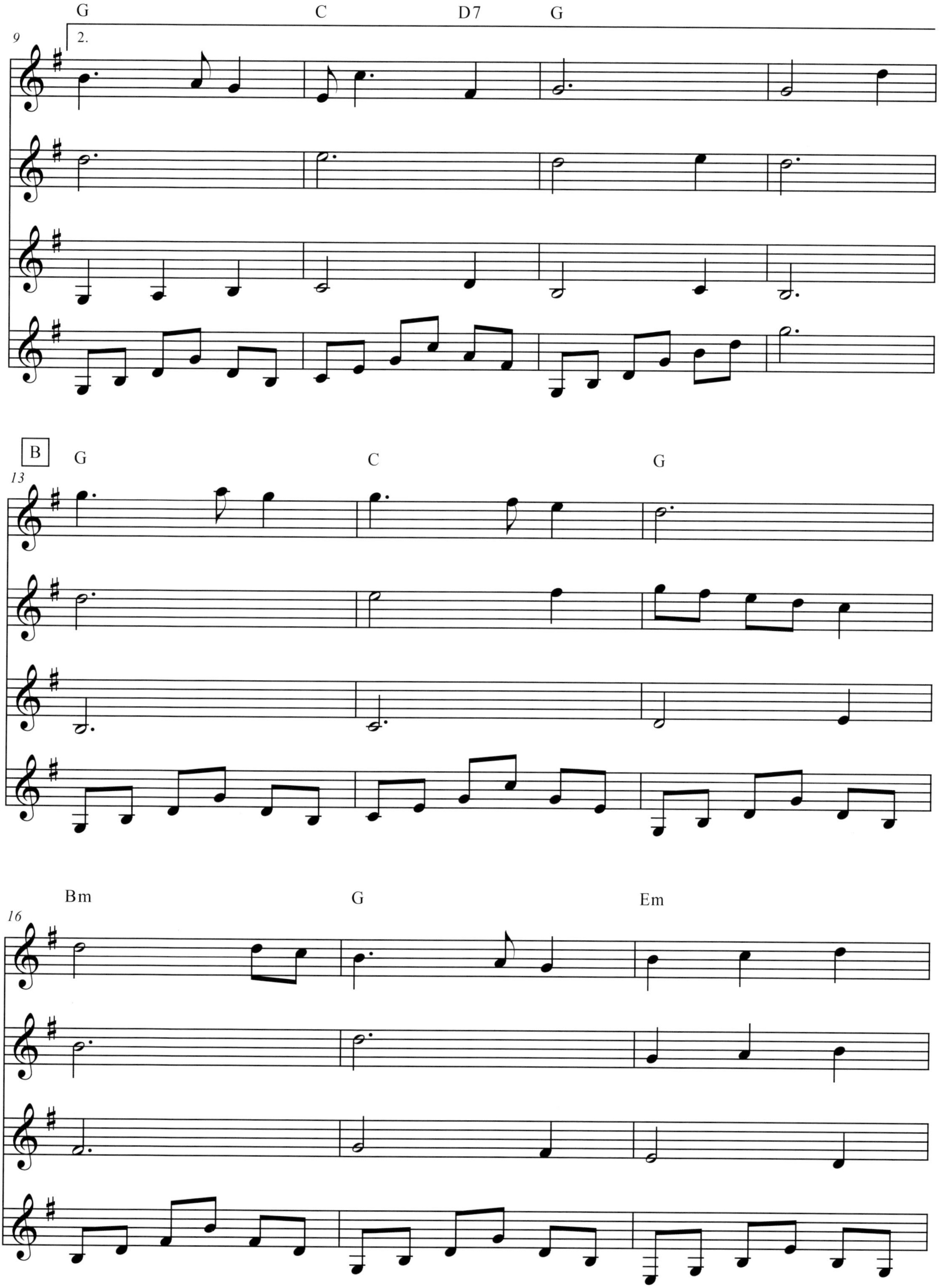
G
C
D7
G
9
2.
B
G
C
G
13
Bm
G
Em
16

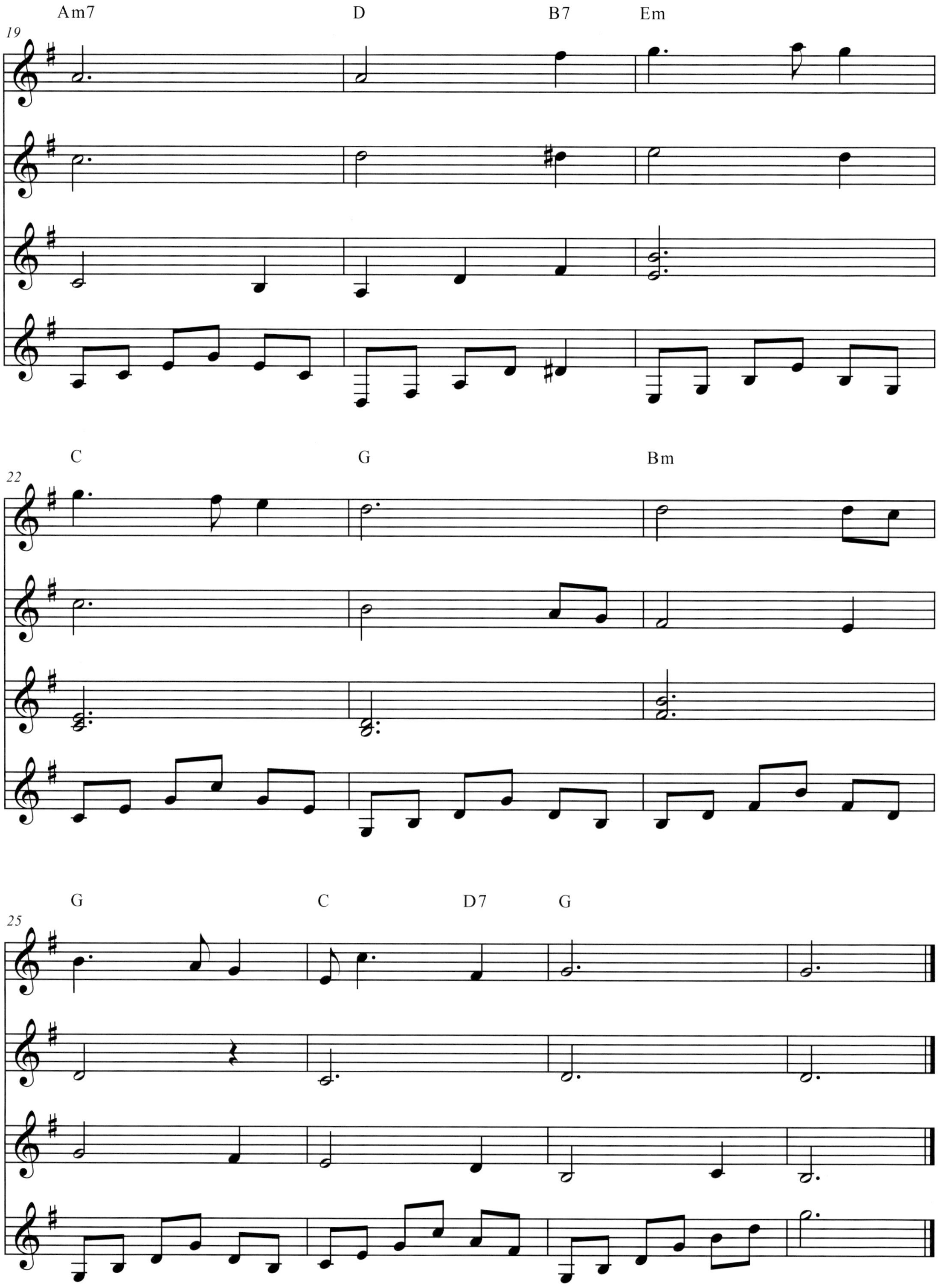
Am7
D
B7
Em
19
C
G
Bm
22
G
C
D7
G
25

Southwind: two-note chords

Ireland: Arranged by© Ken Kolodner

Southwind: with three-note chords

Ireland: Arranged by © Ken Kolodner

It is perhaps a bit tedious to play three-note chords through an entire tune but it is great practice to be able to do so. Three-note chords can be played either LRL or RLR. This harmonization is considerably more adventurous than that which is more commonly played.

Southwind: simple fills

Ireland: Arranged by © Ken Kolodner

Try hammering the fills using alternation. If your hammering seems awkward, make sure you are fully exploring your duplicated notes. Try to play the fills lighter than the melody so that the actual tune is heard above the fills. Using this many fills is a bit much -- what I might call 'over-filling' but it is great practice to learn how to fill using arpeggios.

Southwind: more arranging ideas

Ireland: Arranged by © Ken Kolodner

Some of the ideas presented here are admittedly a bit exploratory and improvisational but that is my intent! I would only play something like this version after firmly establishing the melody played with simpler ideas. Pick and choose as you like.

116

Summer's End

Recorded on Ken Kolodner and Laura Risk's "Roof for the Rain" (2001)

© Ken Kolodner

Summer's End: arrangement #1

Recorded on Ken Kolodner and Laura Risk's "Roof for the Rain" (2001)

Summer's End: arrangement #2

Recorded on Ken Kolodner and Laura Risk's "Roof for the Rain" (2001)

Tennessee Waltz

Pee Wee King and Redd Stewart: Arranged by © Ken Kolodner

Tennessee Waltz: arrangement #1

Pee Wee King and Redd Stewart: Arranged by © Ken Kolodner

Tennessee Waltz: arrangement #2

Pee Wee King and Redd Stewart: Arranged by © Ken Kolodner

Tombigbee's Waltz: melody, harmony & accompaniment

U.S.: Arranged by © Ken Kolodner

Staff line #2 is meant to be played on an instrument capable of sustaining a note (e.g. fiddle or whistle). Note that I sometimes use different bass lines in the harmony and in the backup (e.g. measures 5-8). This tune can easily be played with just three chords (G, C and D). I reserve the use of some of the more radical departures from a standard chord progression for the second or third time through the tune (especially the B7 in measure #24).

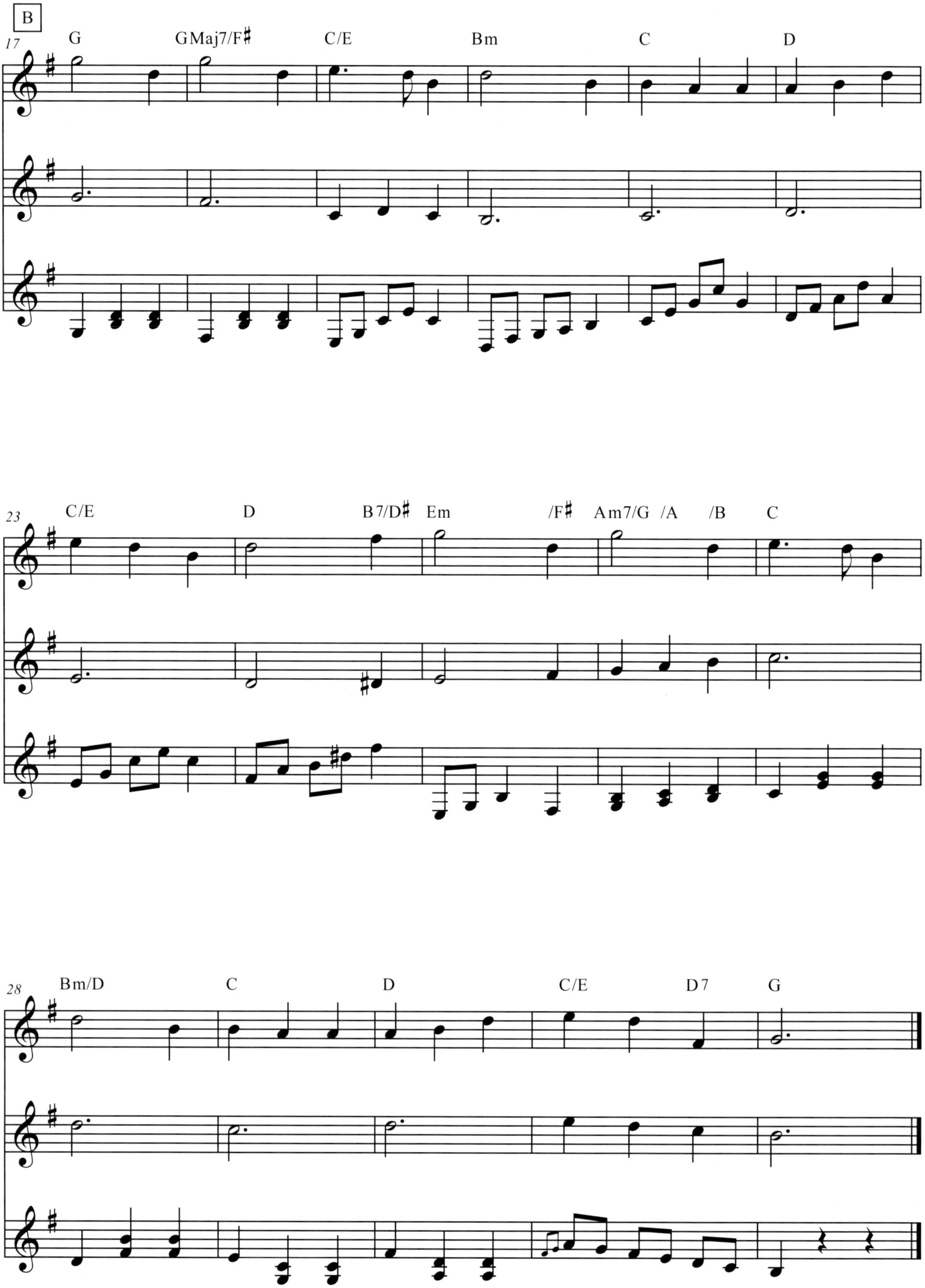
B
17
G GMaj7/F♯ C/E Bm C D
23
C/E D B7/D♯ Em /F♯ Am7/G /A /B C
28
Bm/D C D C/E D7 G

Tombigbee's Waltz: arrangement #1

U.S.: Arranged by © Ken Kolodner

Tombigbee's Waltz: more arranging ideas

U.S.: Arranged by © Ken Kolodner

The 24th of September

Recorded on Greenfire's (Ken Kolodner and Laura Risk) "A Roof for the Rain" (2001)

© Ken Kolodner

The 24th of September: arrangement

Recorded on Greenfire's (Ken Kolodner and Laura Risk) "A Roof for the Rain" (2001)

© Ken Kolodner

Play measures 31-32 to return to the A part

Play these measures to end

Un Canadien Errant: hand separation

(A Wandering Canadian (1842))

Antoine Gerin-Lajoie (1824-1884): Arranged by © Ken Kolodner

Waltz of My Dreams

Recorded on Ken Kolodner's "Journey to the Heartland" (2005) and
on "Hammered Dulcimer Arrangements: Waltzes Vol II" (2005)

Quebec: Arranged by © Ken Kolodner

Use as ending to the A part—this ending is NOT part of the original tune

Waltz of My Dreams: arrangement

Recorded on Ken Kolodner's "Journey to the Heartland" (2005) and
on "Hammered Dulcimer Arrangements: Waltzes Vol II" (2005)

Quebec: Arranged by © Ken Kolodner

Use as an optional ending to the A part (measure 31)—this ending is NOT part of the original tune

APPENDICES

I. INDEX OF TUNES BY TYPE OF TUNE

Slow airs and miscellaneous

Marches

II. INDEX OF TUNES RECORDED BY KEN KOLODNER

Many of the tunes in this volume may be found on YouTube and/or on one of Ken's recordings. Here is a listing of CDs on which the following tunes can be heard.

On Daybreak:
Fanny Power
Margaret Anne Robertson

On Winter Solstice:
Evening of Roses

On Walking Stones:
Carolan's Draught
Caspian Lake
Coleman's March
Cuckoo's Nest
Ian Robertson
Kevin Keegan's
Valse clog Guillemette (The Clock Waltz)

On Helicon:
Da Slockit Light
La Partida

On A Roof for the Rain:
Summer's End
March of the King of Laois
24th of September
Waltz of my Dreams

On Journey to the Heartland:
Black Tail Canyon Waltz, The
Coleman's March
Down Home Waltz, The
My Cape Breton Home
Little Sparrow, The

On Otter Creek:
Bethany Beach

On Out of the Wood:
For Ireland I'd Dare Not Tell Her Name
Lango Lee
Orange Rogue, The
Sir Sydney Smith

On SunRise:
Bonny at Morn
The Cradle Song
Fair Hills of Killen
For Ireland I'd Dare Not Tell Her Name
Forvantan
MacPherson's Lament

On Skipping Rocks:
Cowboy's Waltz
Tombigbee's

III. SELECTED DISCOGRAPHY:

- DAYBREAK, Chris Norman and Ken Kolodner, JEB 001, 1985, re-released 2010, JEB Records, 3806 Fenchurch Rd., Baltimore, MD 21218; 410-243-7254.

- HELICON, Helicon, JEB 002, 1987, Jeb Records.

- THE TITAN, Helicon, DORIAN Discovery, DIS-80115, 1989, re-released, JEB-003, 2006.

- HORIZONS, Helicon, DORIAN Discovery, DIS-80103, 1992.

- WALKING STONES: A Celtic Sojourn, Ken Kolodner with Laura Risk and Robin Bullock, DORIAN, DOR-90248, 1997, re-released FM01, 2006.

- GREENFIRE: A Celtic String Ensemble (Ken Kolodner, Laura Risk and Robin Bullock), DORIAN, DOR-90321, 1998.

- A WINTER SOLSTICE CELEBRATION, Helicon, DORIAN, DOR-90531, 1999.

- A ROOF FOR THE RAIN, Greenfire, (Ken Kolodner, Laura Risk, and guests Keith Murphy and Joseph Sobel) DORIAN, DOR-90598, 2001.

- A JOURNEY TO THE HEARTLAND, Ken Kolodner (with guests Laura Risk, Elke Baker, Robin Bullock, Paddy League) MAGGIE'S MUSIC, MM231, 2005.

- OTTER CREEK, Ken and Brad Kolodner (with guests Elke Baker and Paul Oorts), FENCHURCH MUSIC, FM05, 2011

- SUNRISE, Mark Grobner and Ken Kolodner, SUNRISE MUSIC, 0011, 2011

- OUT OF THE WOOD, Ken Kolodner and Elke Baker (with Brad Kolodner and Eric Eid-Reiner), FENCHURCH MUSIC, FM06, 2011

- SKIPPING ROCKS, Ken and Brad Kolodner (with guests Elke Baker, Alex Lacquement, Kagey Parish, and Robin Bullock), FENCHURCH MUSIC, FM07, 2013

Instructional books/CDs:

- OLD-TIME FIDDLE STYLE: A Collection of 35 Tunes, Ken Kolodner, Catalogue #MB21992BCD Pacific, MO: MEL BAY PUBLICATIONS, August, 2010 (1-800-8MELBAY)

- THE SANDBRIDGE DANCE TUNE COLLECTION: Arrangements for the Hammered Dulcimer, Ken Kolodner, Catalogue #MB30440 Pacific, MO: MEL BAY PUBLICATIONS, September, 2013 (1-800-8MELBAY)

- THE SANDBRIDGE WALTZ AND SLOW AIR COLLECTION: Arrangements for the Hammered Dulcimer, Ken Kolodner, Catalogue #MB30441 Pacific, MO: MEL BAY PUBLICATIONS, November, 2013 (1-800-8MELBAY)

Instructional CDs:

- HAMMERED DULCIMER ARRANGEMENTS: FIDDLE TUNES (REELS), VOLUME I, Ken Kolodner, Fenchurch Music, 2004.

- HAMMERED DULCIMER ARRANGEMENTS: WALTZES AND SLOW TUNES, VOLUME I, Ken Kolodner, Fenchurch Music, 2004.

- HAMMERED DULCIMER ARRANGEMENTS: FIDDLE TUNES (REELS) VOLUME II, Ken Kolodner, Fenchurch Music, 2005.

- HAMMERED DULCIMER ARRANGEMENTS: WALTZES AND SLOW TUNES, VOLUME II, Ken Kolodner, Fenchurch Music, 2005.

- HAMMERED DULCIMER ARRANGEMENTS: SEASONAL MUSIC, VOLUME I, Ken Kolodner, Fenchurch Music, 2005.

IV. ABOUT KEN KOLODNER

Ken Kolodner is recognized as "one of today's most accomplished, musical hammered dulcimer artists...A hammered dulcimer player of great taste and sophistication," (*Elderly*). Ken is known for his improvisational and expressive style that has been described as "nothing short of astonishing" (*The Connection*), "outstanding" (*The New York Times*), "marvelous" (*The Washington Post*), "virtuosic" (*Audio*) "stunning in its musicality" (*Dulcimer Player News*) and "not to be missed" (*USA TODAY*). In more recent years, Ken has received greater recognition as an Old-Time fiddler and in 2010 completed an influential book/CD for *Mel Bay* on Appalachian fiddling.

For over 30 years, Ken toured widely including many years of touring with the world-music trio Helicon (with Chris Norman and Robin Bullock) and with Quebec fiddler Laura Risk. In more recent years, in

Brad and Ken Kolodner in Vermont, 2012 Photo:Hank Schless

addition to much solo work, Ken's playing partners have included Scottish National fiddle champion Elke Baker and Ken's son, clawhammer banjo, guitarist, vocalist and fiddler Brad Kolodner. In 2011, the father-son duo's first release *Otter Creek* featured primarily original and American old time music was the most played instrumental recording on the national Folk Charts in 2011. Performing and recording with his son has been the most satisfying highlight of Ken's performing career. In 2013, father and son released a new CD called *Skipping Rocks*. Among Ken's other credits are *Walking Stones* which sold over 55,000 copes and hit the top of the World Music charts and Helicon's *A Winter Solstice* (1999) which was awarded an "Indie" for Best Seasonal Recording. He has been featured in nationally broadcast concerts on NPR, German National Radio, *The Thistle and the Shamrock*, the CBC, *Performance Today*, *All Things Considered*, and on *The Voice of America*, as well as countless television and radio broadcasts around the U.S. Kolodner was the first American to be featured at the International Hackbrett Festival in Germany and was the featured soloist in an Emmy-nominated CBS-TV Christmas special.

In addition to maintaining 60+ private fiddle and hammered dulcimer students, Ken is one of most highly sought-after teachers of the dulcimer and, more recently the fiddle, having taught at countless festivals and music camps throughout the U.S. Ken now runs his own three week-long master classes in Sandbridge, VA for 50+ intermediate and advanced players from around the U.S. and beyond.

Without any formal music background, Ken began learning to play the fiddle at age 23 by listening to recordings of bluegrass and American Old-Time or Appalachian music. A few years after picking up the fiddle, Ken discovered the hammered dulcimer while in graduate school. Ken's interest in the two instruments developed into an ever-expanding musical appetite beginning with Celtic music and eventually into music spanning many cultures ranging from South American music to Chinese music. While he has mastered the fiddle and hammered dulcimer without formal musical training, he has had plenty of schooling. Along with his hammers, Ken holds a PhD in public health from Johns Hopkins. While most of Ken's professional career is devoted to music, Ken enjoys consulting as a very part-time epidemiologist (with over 100 publications). www.kenkolodner.com

WHAT OTHERS SAY

"…without a doubt, Ken Kolodner is one of the hammered dulcimer's top exponents, playing with a dexterity which would stun many a would-be hammerer." *Folk Tales Magazine*

"When Ken Kolodner plays the hammered dulcimer, something special happens; he makes it sing…inspiring…a tremendous musician…a tremendous album [Journey to the Heartland]…" *Irish Edition, March, 2005.*

"Outstanding…soulfully beautiful." *NY Times*

"…a fiddle and hammered dulcimer virtuoso…just the right amount of fire…totally delightful…"
Sing Out, March 2005

"…joyous…reminiscent of Joe Venuti's work… [Journey to the Heartland] makes for a CD that you can live with all day." *Celtic Beat*

"He's a master at finding what Alasdair Fraser appropriately calls the "rhythmic underbelly" of a tune."
Potomac Valley Fiddle Club Newsletter

"…stirring…evocative…" *The Washington Post, April, 2005.*

"This is just about all anybody could ask for in an instrumental recording. The tunes are all great…Ken's playing positively sizzles …delightful…wonderful… Ken makes great use of syncopation…The up-tempo rhythms are really infectious…" *Dulcimer Player News, 2005*

With Brad Kolodner:

"Father and son have reached that musical telepathy that family members can sometimes achieve. The blend of the hammered dulcimer and banjo is exceptional."
The Old Time Herald January, 2012

"This is old time music played in the purest way: at home, with family, with heart, and with a creative curiosity that lets all listeners know that a passion for traditional music yet thrives in every generation."
Dulcimer Player News April 2011

"Ken Kolodner is a world class multi-instrumentalist…Otter Creek is a joyous recording featuring two fine musicians who playing excellently. There must be something special to that father-son thing.
Sing Out! April, 2011

"Ken is regarded as one of the finest hammered dulcimer players today. What makes this recording special is that Ken collaborates with his son Brad who plays the banjo and banjola. It is what folk music is all about…"
DJ Mark Pederson, WOJB Folkways, Barron, WI

With Laura Risk (Greenfire):

"This is the exceptional group that has raised a standard by both sheer musical expertise, and the love they share which allows for the spontaneous creativity that makes their music special"
The All Music Guide

"The trio plays with the soul, emotion, inspiration, and (when needed) the oomph that should be the envy of many a Celtic band. Greenfire can burn red hot! The repertoire runs the stylistic gamut from hornpipes to polkas to slow airs to jigs to strathspeys, and the geographic gamut from Ireland to Cape Breton to Scotland to Chicago, and even to Finland. Fresh, authentic, invigorating... "
Dirty Linen

"[Greenfire] explores the spirit and soul and mysticism of Irish music and kindred styles... The beauty and the beat of Celtic music are always well served."
The Washington Post

"Exceptional musicians... Greenfire's approach combines a loving respect for tradition and a thoroughly playful sense of creativity. The result is controlled artistry that should appeal to all fans of Celtic music... Clearly this is a 'must have' album for Celtic fans."
Dulcimer Player News

"...inspiring...the interplay between the hammered dulcimer's precise percussive qualities and the graceful fluidity of Risk's fiddling was a real treat."
Rambles: A Cultural Arts Magazine

With Helicon:

"...the multi-instrumental performances of Ken Kolodner and Robin Bullock are virtuosic."
H & B Recordings Direct

"...Quite wonderful! The musicians of Helicon have a deep feeling for an amazing variety of styles. This group is introducing a lot of people to some remarkable music they might not otherwise get to know. They respect the music they play, they play with spirit and sparkle, and they obviously love what they do. So do I. So will you."
Stereo Review

"All three of these guys rank at or near the very top of their profession. The musicianship is uniformly outstanding"
Dulcimer Player News